ALZHEIMER'S DISEASE

MENTAL ILLNESSES AND DISORDERS

MENTAL ILLNESSES AND DISORDERS
Awareness and Understanding

ALZHEIMER'S DISEASE

H.W. Poole

SERIES CONSULTANT
ANNE S. WALTERS, PhD
Chief Psychologist, Emma Pendleton Bradley Hospital
Clinical Associate Professor, Alpert Medical School/Brown University

MC

MASON CREST

Mason Crest
450 Parkway Drive, Suite D
Broomall, PA 19008
www.masoncrest.com

MTM Publishing, Inc.
435 West 23rd Street, #8C
New York, NY 10011
www.mtmpublishing.com

President: Valerie Tomaselli
Vice President, Book Development: Hilary Poole
Designer: Annemarie Redmond
Copyeditor: Peter Jaskowiak
Editorial Assistant: Andrea St. Aubin

Series ISBN: 978-1-4222-3364-1
ISBN: 978-1-4222-3365-8
Ebook ISBN: 978-1-4222-8566-4

Library of Congress Cataloging-in-Publication Data
Poole, Hilary W., author.
  Alzheimer's disease / by H.W. Poole.
     pages cm. — (Mental illnesses and disorders: awareness and understanding)
  Includes bibliographical references and index.
  ISBN 978-1-4222-3365-8 (hardback) — ISBN 978-1-4222-3364-1 (series) — ISBN
978-1-4222-8566-4 (ebook)
  1. Alzheimer's disease— Juvenile literature. I. Title.
  RC523.3.P66 2016
  616.8'31--dc23
                                                                      2015006688

Printed and bound in the United States of America.

9 8 7 6 5 4 3 2

TABLE OF CONTENTS

Key Icons to Look for:

Words to Understand: These words with their easy-to-understand definitions will increase the reader's understanding of the text, while building vocabulary skills.

Sidebars: This boxed material within the main text allows readers to build knowledge, gain insights, explore possibilities, and broaden their perspectives by weaving together additional information to provide realistic and holistic perspectives.

Research Projects: Readers are pointed toward areas of further inquiry connected to each chapter. Suggestions are provided for projects that encourage deeper research and analysis.

Text-Dependent Questions: These questions send the reader back to the text for more careful attention to the evidence presented there.

Series Glossary of Key Terms: This back-of-the-book glossary contains terminology used throughout the series. Words found here increase the reader's ability to read and comprehend higher-level books and articles in this field.

People who cope with mental illnesses and disorders deserve our empathy and respect.

Introduction to the Series

According to the National Institute of Mental Health, in 2012 there were an estimated 45 million people in the United States suffering from mental illness, or 19 percent of all US adults. A separate 2011 study found that among children, almost one in five suffer from some form of mental illness or disorder. The nature and level of impairment varies widely. For example, children and adults with anxiety disorders may struggle with a range of symptoms, from a constant state of worry about both real and imagined events to a complete inability to leave the house. Children or adults with schizophrenia might experience periods when the illness is well controlled by medication and therapies, but there may also be times when they must spend time in a hospital for their own safety and the safety of others. For every person with mental illness who makes the news, there are many more who do not, and these are the people that we must learn more about and help to feel accepted, and even welcomed, in this world of diversity.

It is not easy to have a mental illness in this country. Access to mental health services remains a significant issue. Many states and some private insurers have "opted out" of providing sufficient coverage for mental health treatment. This translates to limits on the amount of sessions or frequency of treatment, inadequate rates for providers, and other problems that make it difficult for people to get the care they need.

Meanwhile, stigma about mental illness remains widespread. There are still whispers about "bad parenting," or "the other side of the tracks." The whisperers imply that mental illness is something you bring upon yourself, or something that someone does to you. Obviously, mental illness can be exacerbated by an adverse event such as trauma or parental instability. But there is just as much truth to the biological bases of mental illness. No one is made schizophrenic by ineffective parenting, for example, or by engaging in "wild" behavior as an adolescent. Mental illness is a complex interplay of genes, biology, and the environment, much like many physical illnesses.

People with mental illness are brave soldiers, really. They fight their illness every day, in all of the settings of their lives. When people with an anxiety disorder graduate from college, you know that they worked very hard to get there—harder, perhaps, than those who did not struggle with a psychiatric issue. They got up every day with a pit in their stomach about facing the world, and they worried about their finals more than their classmates. When they had to give a presentation in class, they thought their world was going to end and that they would faint, or worse, in front of everyone. But they fought back, and they kept going. Every day. That's bravery, and that is to be respected and congratulated.

These books were written to help young people get the facts about mental illness. Facts go a long way to dispel stigma. Knowing the facts gives students the opportunity to help others to know and understand. If your student lives with someone with mental illness, these books can help students know a bit more about what to expect. If they are concerned about someone, or even about themselves, these books are meant to provide some answers and a place to start.

The topics covered in this series are those that seem most relevant for middle schoolers—disorders that they are most likely to come into contact with or to be curious about. Schizophrenia is a rare illness, but it is an illness with many misconceptions and inaccurate portrayals in media. Anxiety and depressive disorders, on the other hand, are quite common. Most of our youth have likely had personal experience of anxiety or depression, or knowledge of someone who struggles with these symptoms.

As a teacher or a librarian, thank you for taking part in dispelling myths and bringing facts to your children and students. Thank you for caring about the brave soldiers who live and work with mental illness. These reference books are for all of them, and also for those of us who have the good fortune to work with and know them.

—Anne S. Walters, PhD
Chief Psychologist, Emma Pendleton Bradley Hospital
Clinical Professor, Alpert Medical School/Brown University

CHAPTER ONE

WHAT ARE COGNITIVE DISORDERS?

Words to Understand

cognitive: having to do with thought and perception.

deficiency: a lack of something.

dementia: a mental disorder, featuring severe memory loss.

stroke: rupture of an artery in the brain.

panic attack: a short period of intense fear.

Do your grandparents repeat themselves or forget things? Maybe every Thanksgiving, your grandmother tells the same story about that time she burned the turkey. Or maybe you have to remind your grandfather of your best friend's name, even though he's met your friend a number of times before.

When we are young, our brains are very good at storing information. When we learn something, our brains develop new pathways to save the new item. When we get older, those pathways become less efficient. It becomes harder to store new information.

As people age, learning new things can become challenging.

This is a natural part of aging. It can be frustrating sometimes—both for the aging person and the people who love her. But a poor memory alone is not a disease.

AROUND THE WORLD

According to the World Health Organization (WHO), about 35.6 million people around the world were living with some form of dementia in 2010. That number is expected to almost double every 20 years. The WHO also says that one case of dementia is diagnosed every 4 seconds.

More Than Forgetful

Unfortunately, sometimes memory loss goes beyond telling the same story a few times. Sometimes more serious **cognitive** issues—such as forgetting basic facts about oneself—occur as we age. There are a number of mental problems that are grouped together and called cognitive disorders. The best known of these is Alzheimer's disease, which is a form of **dementia**.

In Alzheimer's disease, cells are destroyed in the area of the brain that controls thinking and memory. Eventually cells in other brain areas are also destroyed. The disease is progressive, which means that the person will gradually get worse.

One of the most common early symptoms of Alzheimer's is memory loss. At first, this involves a person's short-term memory of things that happened within the last few minutes or hours. For example, someone with Alzheimer's may forget what he

DID YOU KNOW?

Dementia can be caused by conditions other than Alzheimer's. However, because Alzheimer's and dementia are so closely related, people sometimes use the words to mean the same thing.

A common saying about Alzheimer's is that it is not about forgetting your keys, but about putting your keys in the freezer. In other words, Alzheimer's can make people lose track of the logical connections between different things.

just had for breakfast. Or he may not remember what day of the month it is, even a few minutes after someone tells him. The same person, however, may remember his childhood in detail.

As with other dementias, symptoms include problems with reasoning or judgment, difficulty in learning anything new, loss of language skills, and the inability to do everyday things. For example, someone with this disease might put her watch in the refrigerator and the lettuce in the bathroom.

The disease can also cause personality changes. Sometimes a person with Alzheimer's becomes confrontational and angry. Other times, she sees things that are not there or believes in a reality that does not exist.

Other Types of Dementia

Alzheimer's disease is the most common type of dementia. It is also one of the leading causes of death in North America. But the problems associated with other cognitive disorders are just as devastating. For example, vascular dementia is the second most common cognitive disorder. It is caused by a series of small **strokes** within the brain that may or may not be noticed when they happen. As with Alzheimer's, brain matter is destroyed, affecting memory and other functions.

There are two cognitive problems that are fairly similar to Alzheimer's. One is called mild cognitive impairment (MCI). This condition has the same symptoms as Alzheimer's, but

Dementia has a huge impact on entire families.

Deaths from Alzheimer's Disease: 2000 to 2010

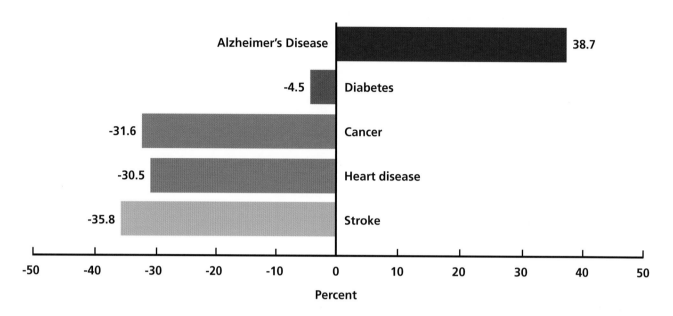

In the United States, rates from Alzheimer's increased more than 38 percent between 2000 and 2010. The number of deaths from other diseases declined in that same period.

they are not nearly as severe. MCI can sometimes turn into Alzheimer's, but it doesn't always.

Another Alzheimer-like condition is mild neurocognitive disorder (MND). This condition involves a decline in memory and learning, attention span, language, or motor skills that is abnormal for the person's age. MND is usually caused by some other problem—for instance, a person might be diagnosed with MND due to brain injury.

Parkinson's disease is a progressive disease that causes stiff muscles, tremors, shuffling movements, and eventually dementia. Parkinson's disease is most common in the elderly, but it can also occur in much younger people. For example, the actor Michael J. Fox, who suffers from this disease, has become a spokesperson for Parkinson's.

Huntington's disease is an inherited, genetic disease. People with Huntington's often have involuntary dance-like movements, clumsiness, slurred speech, short-term memory loss, and depression. Symptoms usually begin after the age of 35. The child of someone with Huntington's has a 50 percent chance of inheriting the disease. Although there is no cure for Huntington's, treating the symptoms can make it easier to live with.

The category of dementia includes many diseases. Some, like Alzheimer's, Parkinson's, and Huntington's, have no cure. But other dementias can be stopped or reversed. If cognitive problems are caused by drug use, depression, thyroid disease, or a vitamin B12 **deficiency**, real improvement can occur after

Occasionally, dementia symptoms are caused by a deficiency in vitamin B12. This problem can be solved by changes in diet or by injections of B12.

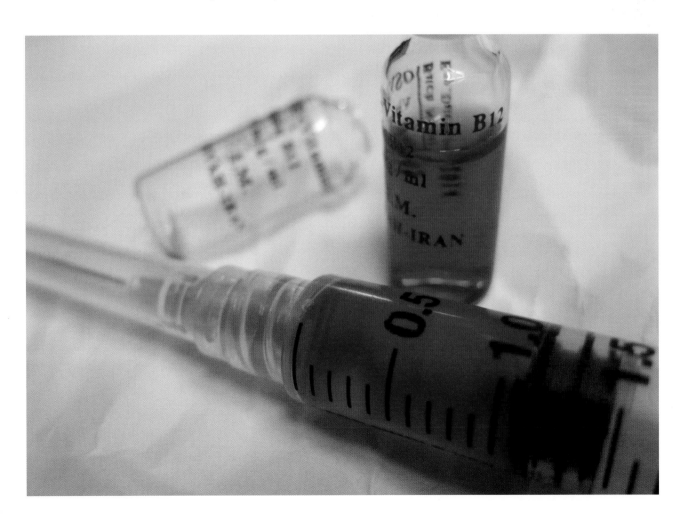

medical treatment. Unfortunately, these curable dementias only represent about 5 percent of people with the disease.

Loss of memory, personality changes, and an inability to perform normal activities are all very stressful. On top of all this, the individual may become depressed, anxious, or experience **panic attacks**. Other people may become aggressive, either verbally or physically. Unfortunately, these emotional symptoms can make the other symptoms get worse faster. The good news is that, in many cases, medications can help control these problems. Researchers have also developed medications that can actually improve memory.

Text-Dependent Questions

1. What are the different types of cognitive disorders?
2. Which types may be curable?
3. What causes vascular dementia?

Research Project

Pick one of the other cognitive disorders, such as Parkinson's disease or Huntington's disease, and write a history of it. When was it discovered, and by whom? Is there a difference between how it was once treated and how it is treated now?

CHAPTER TWO

UNDERSTANDING ALZHEIMER'S

Words to Understand

autopsy: an examination of a body to determine the cause of death.

cerebral cortex: the outer portion of the brain.

correlation: a relationship or connection.

denial: refusal to admit that there is a problem.

theorize: to suggest ideas or conclusions about something.

Scientists do not completely understand what happens inside the brain when someone has Alzheimer's disease—but researchers are looking for the answers.

Background

The disease is named for German physician Alois Alzheimer, who was the first to study it. In 1906, Dr. Alzheimer performed an **autopsy** on a woman who had suffered from dementia. He noticed two abnormal structures in her brain. One is called *plaques*—these are clumps of protein fragments that accumulate outside brain cells. The other is called *tangles*. These are clumps of altered proteins inside

A close-up of the neurons of a person with Alzheimer's. The light areas are called amyloid plaques; these are sticky clumps that build up on the neurons and interfere with their functioning.

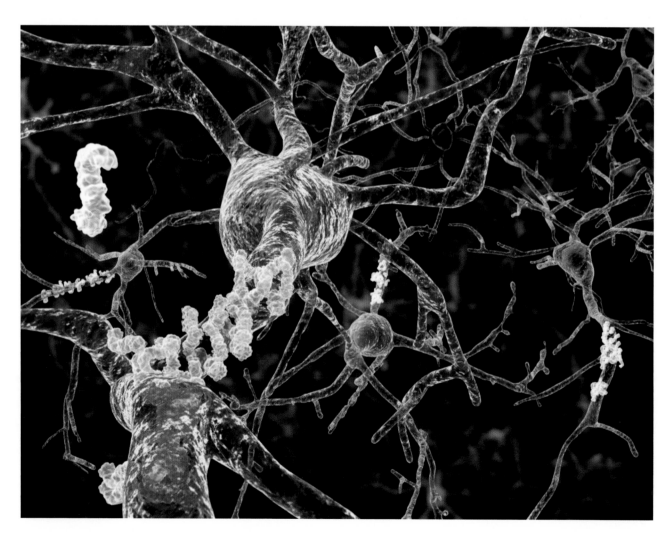

GENDER AND ALZHEIMER'S

Women are more likely to develop Alzheimer's than men. A woman has about a 1 in 6 chance of developing Alzheimer's, as opposed to a man, who has about a 1 in 11 chance. However, this is partly because women simply live longer than men.

the cells. The presence of plaques and tangles is evidence of Alzheimer's disease.

The **cerebral cortex** is where thought processes take place. In a normal brain, the nerve cells are arranged in an orderly way, but in the brain of an Alzheimer's patient, the cells become disorganized. It's as if nerve cells in the cerebral cortex and other regions of the brain were attacked by a deadly enemy. The formations of plaques and tangles start to take over more and more of the brain. As Dr. Alzheimer first noticed, the cells are bunched up like a rope tied in knots. As the cells are attacked and killed, the person's symptoms will get worse.

One of the strange aspects of the plaques and tangles is that they only develop in the parts of the brain that control memory. That's why people with the early stages of Alzheimer's may be very healthy in every other way. Sometimes the tangles and plaques have been found in the brains of healthy aging persons who did not show any symptoms of a cognitive disorder.

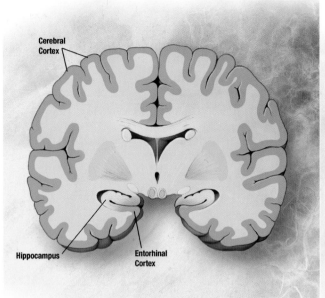
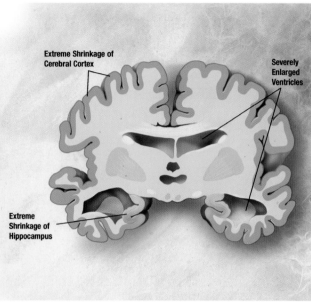

Cerebral Cortex

Extreme Shrinkage of Cerebral Cortex

Severely Enlarged Ventricles

Extreme Shrinkage of Hippocampus

Hippocampus

Entorhinal Cortex

A comparison of a healthy brain and a brain with Alzheimer's.

Inside the Brain

A healthy brain sends messages throughout the nervous system by way of *neurons*. The neurons pass along the messages, similar to the way a bucket brigade hands along a bucket of water. The neurons are not connected to each other; there is a small gap between each one called a *synapse*. Messages move across the gaps by way of chemicals called *neurotransmitters*. These chemicals are "caught" by part of the neuron called the *receptor*.

In searching for the cause of Alzheimer's, scientists have studied both neurotransimtters and receptors. In the brain of someone with Alzheimer's, the neuron receptors show abnormalities. Scientists believe these abnormalities may actually change the messages as they move from neuron to neuron. Imagine that you're playing the game "Telephone," where you whisper a message down

DID YOU KNOW?

According to the Alzheimer's Association, about 1 in 9 people over age 65 has Alzheimer's disease.

a long line of people. If someone can't hear very well or can't speak very well, the message is distorted—and what the last person in the line hears may be totally different from the message spoken by the first person in the line. That's a little like what happens in the brains of people with Alzheimer's (and other cognitive disorders). The messages passed along by the neurons get mixed up or confused.

SYMPTOMS

According to the Alzheimer's Association, there are 10 "warning signs" of early Alzheimer's disease:

- memory loss that disrupts daily life
- difficulty solving problems
- difficulty completing tasks that should be familiar
- confusing time or place
- trouble understanding visual information (such as judging distance or identifying colors)
- problems with writing or speaking that didn't exist before
- misplacing things
- poor decision making
- withdrawing from friends and social activities
- changes in mood (such as becoming upset easily, or getting depressed or suspicious)

The tricky part is, many of these symptoms are common among all older people to some degree. It is not always easy to tell the difference between "normal" aging and a cognitive problem. This is why it's important to discuss symptoms with a medical professional.

DEALING WITH DENIAL

One difficult aspect of Alzheimer's disease is that many people who have it do not want to admit that there is a problem. This **denial** is understandable. But it is also unfortunate, because medications to treat Alzheimer's are more effective if they are given early. When it comes to Alzheimer's treatment, the sooner, the better.

If you are concerned about an older relative or friend, it's best to discuss it with a parent or other trusted adult. It is probably not a good idea to bring up the subject with the person, as this is likely to be upsetting. But don't keep your worries to yourself, either! Talk to an adult about what concerns you.

Causes and Correlations

We know a lot about what is going wrong in the brains of people with Alzheimer's. As mentioned above, there can be problems with neurotransmitters and receptors, and plaques and tangles can develop in the brain. But researchers are still struggling to figure out exactly what causes these things to go wrong in the first place. There is still no definite answer. However, we do know some things about who is more likely to develop the disease.

Genetics. Researchers have identified certain genes that are associated with Alzheimer's. But problems with these genes can only explain about 5 percent of Alzheimer's cases.

Family History. It is possible to have a family history of Alzheimer's without actually having those particular genes. Doctors are not entirely sure, at this stage, why this is so. Still, research suggests that someone with an Alzheimer's patient in his immediate family has a 40 to 50 percent chance of developing the disease himself. So while family history is a factor, it does not seem to be the only one.

Physical Health. People with high blood pressure, high cholesterol, or diabetes seem to have a greater likelihood of also developing Alzheimer's. Smoking and lack of exercise also appear to play a negative role.

It is important to understand that these factors have what scientists call a **correlation** with Alzheimer's. That is, they are associated with the disease—many people who have one also have the other. No one has proven, however, that they

Alzheimer's disease can run in families.

are direct *causes* of the disease. So, for example, just because someone has high blood pressure, it does not automatically mean she will develop Alzheimer's later.

Lifestyle. Elderly people who stay active—not only in the physical sense, but also mentally—seem to be able to avoid Alzheimer's for a longer period of time. Hobbies like reading, doing crossword puzzles, or playing a musical instrument are good ways to keep the brain busy and engaged. Whenever we learn something new, we build new connections in our brains. Scientists **theorize** that the more the brain is used, the less likely it is to decline. People who have challenging

Experts believe that keeping active is a good way to ward off dementia.

jobs or busy social lives seem to do better in avoiding or at
least delaying Alzheimer's.

Text-Dependent Questions

1. Who discovered the disease, and how?
2. What theories do doctors have about what causes Alzheimer's disease?
3. Name some symptoms of the disease.

Research Project

Find out more about the warning signs of Alzheimer's. Look at some of the
following websites for information:

- Alzheimer's Association: www.alz.org.
- Alzheimer's Foundation of America: www.alzfdn.org.
- Alzheimer Mexico, I.A.P.: www.alzheimermexico.org.mx/.
- Alzheimer Society of Canada: www.alzheimer.ca/en.
- National Institute on Aging, Alzheimer's Disease Education and Referral
  Center: www.nia.nih.gov/alzheimers.

Collect a list of signs and symptoms to look for. What do the various groups
recommend that someone with those symptoms should do next?

CHAPTER THREE

TREATMENT

Words to Understand

conclusive: definite.

enhancer: something that makes something else better.

simulate: to copy or represent something else.

So far, there is no cure for Alzheimer's disease. Researchers are working very hard to find one, and the need is quite urgent. By 2050, as many as 16 million people may have the disease. In the meantime, there are many medications available that can ease the symptoms. Others have the potential to slow down the course of the disease, especially if they are given early.

Drugs to Treat Memory Loss

At the end of the 20th century, researchers announced they had developed a drug to improve memory, attention, and decision-making abilities in people with Alzheimer's disease.

There are a number of medicines that can help Alzheimer's patients.

RULING THINGS OUT

Before an Alzheimer's diagnosis is made, a doctor will recommend various tests, to make sure that some other medical condition is not creating the problems. These tests may include:

- blood tests
- thyroid function tests
- tests for infectious diseases
- tests to determine vitamin levels in the blood
- an electroencephalogram (EEG), which measures brain waves
- an electrocardiogram (ECG), which measures the electrical activity of the heart
- cranial scans, which look at the structures of the brain
- a spinal tap, in which a small amount of fluid is withdrawn from the spinal column to look for infection or bleeding

The results of the study were presented in Stockholm, Sweden, in April 2000. The study indicated that a drug called galantamine hydrobromide helped patients in the early stages of the disease. These patients had better impulse control, and they could better handle everyday tasks (such as dressing, washing, and feeding themselves). Perhaps best of all, they had better language skills, memory, and decision-making abilities. The effects lasted for as long as 12 months.

Galantamine (with a trade name of Reminyl) was approved for use in the United States in April 2001. It is called a cognitive **enhancer**. There are other cognitive enhancers available, as well. They offer the most hope of any drugs developed so far to treat Alzheimer's.

Doctors and scientists have found that another class of drugs, including one called memantine, sometimes help patients with late-stage Alzheimer's. But memantine only relieves symptoms like memory loss; it does not reverse the course of the disease.

The search continues for a drug that will heal human memory. In the search for memory-enhancing drugs, some researchers are experimenting on rats. They use metal electrodes to send tiny jolts of electricity into rat brains. The zap of electricity **simulates** what happens in brain cells whenever a new memory is created in the brain. At the same time, experimental drugs drip into the brain cells of the rat, while other electrodes measure any changes in the cell activity. Researchers are looking for chemicals that will help the neurons form stronger connections that last longer. The hope is that a medicine can be developed to improve human memory.

How Cognitive Enhancers Work

Reminyl, along with other cognitive enhancers (with names like Cognex, Aricept, and Exelon), are all designed to improve memory, attention, and decision-making abilities.

Research has shown that people with Alzheimer's don't have enough of certain neurotransmitters in their brains.

Researchers are still looking for a drug that can reverse the damage that the disease does to the brain.

Without these, the human brain does not work properly. Cognitive enhancers result in higher concentrations of missing neurotransmitters. This leads to improved communication between the nerve cells, which temporarily improves symptoms. These medicines are also used to treat other cognitive problems, such as Parkinson's disease. They have even been used successfully in some people with schizophrenia.

A cognitive disorder is caused by things beyond anyone's control. When things go wrong inside the brain, there is never a simple way to "fix" the problem. Cognitive enhancers and other drugs, however, have the power to change the way the brain works. They cannot make the problem disappear, but they can reduce its symptoms.

Alternative Treatments

Many people with Alzheimer's (or who love someone with the disease) look beyond traditional medicine for help. This is very understandable! So far, traditional medicine can only slow down Alzheimer's, but not cure it. It makes sense that people would want to try just about anything to get better.

A number of different vitamins and herbs have been suggested. One is Vitamin E, which is believed to help the body heal itself. Another is ginkgo biloba, an herb that is believed to improve memory. Coconut oil, calcium taken from coral, and omega-3 supplements are just a few things people have tried to ward off Alzheimer's (see sidebar on page 33).

There are a few potential problems with these approaches, though. First, herbal remedies and vitamins are not regulated by the government. This means you can't know for sure whether the supplements are pure or not. Many of them have not been studied in a scientific setting to prove their effectiveness. Or, if they have been studied, the results are not **conclusive**. For example, some German studies found that ginkgo biloba improved the memory of older

DID YOU KNOW?

More than 40 percent of Americans in assisted living or "rest homes" have Alzheimer's disease.

people; but researchers in the United States have not agreed with those findings.

And finally, many elderly people have more than one health problem. Someone might have Alzheimer's and diabetes. In that case, it's important to consider how any drug or supplement will impact the whole person. For example, high doses of vitamin E can be toxic. Vitamin E can also reduce the effectiveness of medicine taken to lower cholesterol. For many older people, keeping cholesterol low is extremely important. For those people, vitamin E could hurt more than it helps.

That said, a lot depends on the person. Someone with naturally low cholesterol might benefit from carefully

Some people take vitamin E in hopes of warding off dementia. However, vitamin E can interfere with other medicines, so it's important to check with your doctor.

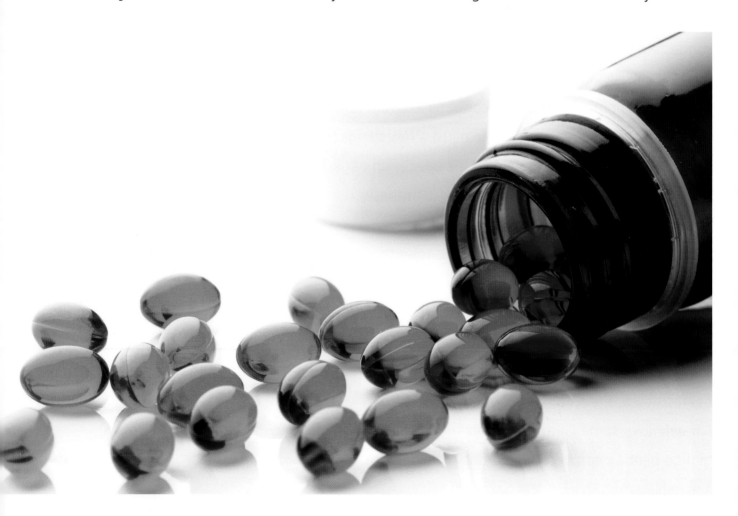

BUYER BEWARE

A diagnosis of Alzheimer's can be terrifying—to the person who has it, and to the people who love that person. This can make people too willing to believe empty promises. It's fairly easy for dishonest companies to say they've found a "miracle drug." Many people, desperate to save their loved ones or themselves, are all too ready to believe.

For example, a product called coral calcium, which is supposedly made from the shells found on coral reefs, has been marketed as a cure for Alzheimer's disease. But there is no scientific evidence to back up this claim. In fact, the US government has filed complaints against coral calcium companies for making false claims about their products.

Hopefully, someday there will be a real miracle that cures Alzheimer's. Until then, be suspicious of anyone who claims to have a magic pill that will solve the problem.

managed vitamin E supplements. The point here is not that alternative medicines are all bad. Rather, the point is simply that, any and all medication—alternative or not—should be discussed with a doctor.

Alzheimer's and Depression

People with Alzheimer's disease frequently suffer from depression as well. People in the early stages of Alzheimer's might feel anxious and embarrassed about their symptoms. They might feel guilty that they are causing their family so much difficulty. These feelings are all to be expected. But sometimes that sadness drags on and on, resulting in a serious depression. If someone is seriously depressed, then the depression needs to be treated.

Depression can be a big problem for people with dementia.

Depression and other mood issues should not be considered "normal" for a person who is getting older. No one, including the elderly, should suffer with psychiatric symptoms when treatment is available. Treating elderly people with any drugs, but especially psychiatric ones, requires much effort by the physician, the patient, and often a caretaker. All physical problems must be monitored.

Some physicians are so concerned about the possible side effects of medications that they do not treat mood problems in elderly patients. Other doctors, however, are now convinced that people with cognitive disorders do not need to be depressed or anxious, too. After a physical and mental evaluation, these physicians will often prescribe either an antianxiety medication or an antidepressant. These drugs help the brain work more efficiently to overcome depression. People may find relief from the depression that had made their memory symptoms worse.

Text-Dependent Questions

1. What is a cognitive enhancer, and how does it work?
2. What tests might a doctor give someone before diagnosing Alzheimer's? Why are these tests given?
3. What can be done to help a depressed person with Alzheimer's?

Research Project

Find out more about depression and what can be done about it. Make a list of things someone who is depressed might do to feel better—include things that people can do on their own.

CHAPTER FOUR

COPING WITH ALZHEIMER'S

 Words to Understand

essential: completely important and necessary.

majority: an amount more than half of the total number.

Medicare: government health care program for people over age 64.

If you have a relative with Alzheimer's, you are definitely not alone. More than 5 million people currently have the disease. The vast **majority** of them are over age 65, but about 200,000 people under age 65 have the disease. According to the Alzheimer's Association, in 2013, about 15.5 million family members helped care for someone with the illness.

What Do I Do?

Alzheimer's can be both scary and frustrating. We all want our parents and grandparents to take care of *us*—yet we may suddenly find ourselves caring for *them*. It is not easy to

Socializing is an important way to keep people with Alzheimer's engaged with the world.

know what to do. Here are some tips on what you can do if someone you care about has Alzheimer's:

- **Try to be patient**. This is very easy to say and not so easy to do. But people with Alzheimer's need a lot of patience. Let's say you want to play a game with your relative. Explain the rules slowly, one rule at a time. Don't be surprised if you need to go over the rules more than once. If you're telling a story, tell it step by step, rather than telling the whole story quickly. Try not to get upset if you have to repeat some parts.

- **Keep things simple**. When spending time with someone who has Alzheimer's, it can help to limit distractions. For example, if you want to have a conversation, turn off the TV. If you are making a snack, offer two choices instead of five.

- **Move around, if at all possible**. If your relative is healthy enough, going on a walk can be a great activity. You don't have to go fast, and you don't have to go anywhere in particular. It could just be around the backyard. If it's a nice day, you and an adult could take your relative to the park. If it's a rainy day, maybe you could go to the mall. The point is just to be with the person and to get him or her moving around a little bit.

    However, make sure that your parent or other trusted adult is never too far away. It's great to get outside, but you don't want to become lost or overwhelmed.

- **Put yourself in the other person's shoes**. People with Alzheimer's sometimes get upset easily. Sometimes

Opposite page: Going for a walk is a great way to spend time with a loved one who has dementia.

A person with dementia is still the same person he or she was before.

they say things they don't really mean. This might be because they are depressed or anxious, as discussed in chapter two. Other times they are just angry.

Think about it: Wouldn't you be angry? What if you woke up one day and found that you could no longer remember how to play your favorite game, or even how to tie your shoes? What if you couldn't even recognize these people who are suddenly in your house, ordering you around? You'd probably be mad, too.

- **Remember, the disease is not the person**. Speaking of being mad, you might be mad yourself, just because of the situation your relative is in. Charlene Brocklebank, who is project manager of Mental Health Connections in Windsor, Ontario, calls Alzheimer's disease "the thief." Slowly but surely, Alzheimer's steals away the person you love. It's okay to be mad about that sometimes, too.

But it's also important to remember that Alzheimer's disease is just that, a disease. It's a physical problem in the brain. If your relative frustrates you—maybe he can't remember things, or he can't recognize you, or he says something unkind—remember that he's not doing it on purpose.

Think of it this way: if your relative had cancer, you wouldn't be mad at him. In fact, you would do everything you could to help. Alzheimer's is no different. It does *seem* different, because you are dealing with the brain, rather than the lungs or other organs. But in the end, "the thief" is just a physical illness. Even if he can't express it, your relative still loves you just as much as before.

THE COST OF ALZHEIMER'S

Alzheimer's is the most expensive disease in the United States. Almost one-fifth of all **Medicare** spending is devoted to taking care of Alzheimer's patients.

According to the Alzheimer's Association, taking care of people with the disease cost about $200 billion in 2012. The group projects that the United States will spend more than $1 trillion a year on Alzheimer's care by 2050.

As Things Get Worse

Scientists are racing to find a cure for Alzheimer's. And, as mentioned in chapter three, drugs called cognitive enhancers can help slow down the disease. But for now, the sad truth is that the mind of someone with Alzheimer's will continue to decline.

The person may reach a point where she no longer lives in the now, but moves further back in time. In her mind, she may travel back to childhood. Experts will tell you that there is no use in trying to argue with the person. It is better to try and accept who the person is now. Constantly correcting her won't

Eventually, someone with Alzheimer's will need care in a hospital, nursing home, or hospice setting.

fix anything; it will just be upsetting. Acceptance and love give peace to everyone involved.

Try and recognize the strengths that your relative still has. A person with Alzheimer's can no longer do many things. But she will still be able to do other things. Someone whose mind is failing is a lot like a little kid: both need a lot of help, but they also need to feel included and valued. And both have a lot to contribute to the family, even if their contributions are different from what they were before.

Our memories are an **essential** part of who we are. That's why Alzheimer's is so painful—it is the thief that steals our memories away. But we do not need memory to love and be loved.

Text-Dependent Questions

1. About how many people in the United States have Alzheimer's?
2. Why is it so important to be patient with people with Alzheimer's, and why is that so hard to do?
3. What are some things you might do to help someone with Alzheimer's?

Research Project

Visit the websites listed in the back of this book to find out more about caring for someone with Alzheimer's. See what other pieces of advice you can find to help family members cope. Which pieces of advice make sense to you; which ones do not?

Further Reading

BOOKS

Castleman, Michael, Dolores Gallagher-Thompson, and Matthew Naythons. *There's Still a Person in There.* New York: G. P. Putnam's Sons, 1999.

Landau, Elaine. *Alzheimer's: A Forgotten Life.* New York: Franklin Watts, 2005.

Mace, Nancy L., and Peter V. Rabins. *The 36-Hour Day: A Family Guide for Caring for People Who Have Alzheimer's Disease.* 5th ed. Baltimore, MD: Johns Hopkins University Press, 2011.

ONLINE

Alzheimer's Association. www.alz.org.

Alzheimer's Disease Education and Referral Center. www.nia.nih.gov/alzheimers.

Alzheimer Society of Canada. www.alzheimer.ca.

Institute for Memory Impairments and Neurological Disorders (UCI MIND). www.alz.uci.edu.

Latino Alzheimer's and Memory Disorders Alliance. http://www.latinoalzheimersalliance.org.

LOSING HOPE?

This free, confidential phone number will connect you to counselors who can help.

National Suicide Prevention Lifeline

1-800-273-TALK (1-800-273-8255)

Series Glossary

acute: happening powerfully for a short period of time.

affect: as a noun, the way someone seems on the outside—including attitude, emotion, and voice (pronounced with the emphasis on the first syllable, "AFF-eckt").

atypical: different from what is usually expected.

bipolar: involving two, opposite ends.

chronic: happening again and again over a long period of time.

comorbidity: two or more illnesses appearing at the same time.

correlation: a relationship or connection.

delusion: a false belief with no connection to reality.

dementia: a mental disorder, featuring severe memory loss.

denial: refusal to admit that there is a problem.

depressant: a substance that slows down bodily functions.

depression: a feeling of hopelessness and lack of energy.

deprivation: a hurtful lack of something important.

diagnose: to identify a problem.

empathy: understanding someone else's situation and feelings.

epidemic: a widespread illness.

euphoria: a feeling of extreme, even overwhelming, happiness.

hallucination: something a person sees or hears that is not really there.

heredity: the passing of a trait from parents to children.

hormone: a substance in the body that helps it function properly.

hypnotic: a type of drug that causes sleep.

impulsivity: the tendency to act without thinking.

inattention: distraction; not paying attention.

insomnia: inability to fall asleep and/or stay asleep.

licensed: having an official document proving one is capable with a certain set of skills.

manic: a high level of excitement or energy.

misdiagnose: to incorrectly identify a problem.

moderation: limited in amount, not extreme.

noncompliance: refusing to follow rules or do as instructed.

onset: the beginning of something; pronounced like "on" and "set."

outpatient: medical care that happens while a patient continues to live at home.

overdiagnose: to determine more people have a certain illness than actually do.

pediatricians: doctors who treat children and young adults.

perception: awareness or understanding of reality.

practitioner: a person who actively participates in a particular field.

predisposition: to be more likely to do something, either due to your personality or biology.

psychiatric: having to do with mental illness.

psychiatrist: a medical doctor who specializes in mental disorders.

psychoactive: something that has an effect on the mind and behavior.

psychosis: a severe mental disorder where the person loses touch with reality.

psychosocial: the interaction between someone's thoughts and the outside world of relationships.

psychotherapy: treatment for mental disorders.

relapse: getting worse after a period of getting better.

spectrum: a range; in medicine, from less extreme to more extreme.

stereotype: a simplified idea about a type of person, not connected to actual individuals.

stimulant: a substance that speeds up bodily functions.

therapy: treatment of a problem; can be done with medicine or simply by talking with a therapist.

trigger: something that causes something else.

Index

Page numbers in *italics* refer to photographs.

About the Author

H. W. POOLE is a writer and editor of books for young people, such as the *Horrors of History* series (Charlesbridge). She is also responsible for many critically acclaimed reference books, including *Political Handbook of the World* (CQ Press) and the *Encyclopedia of Terrorism* (SAGE). She was coauthor and editor of the *History of the Internet* (ABC-CLIO), which won the 2000 American Library Association RUSA award.

About the Advisor

ANNE S. WALTERS is Clinical Associate Professor of Psychiatry and Human Behavior. She is the Clinical Director of the Children's Partial Hospital Program at Bradley Hospital, a program that provides partial hospital level of care for children ages 7–12 and their families. She also serves as Chief Psychologist for Bradley Hospital. She is actively involved in teaching activities within the Clinical Psychology Training Programs of the Alpert Medical School of Brown University and serves as Child Track Seminar Co-Coordinator. Dr. Walters completed her undergraduate work at Duke University, graduate school at Georgia State University, internship at UTexas Health Science Center, and postdoctoral fellowship at Brown University. Her interests lie in the area of program development, treatment of severe psychiatric disorders in children, and psychotic spectrum disorders.

Photo Credits

Photos are for illustrative purposes only; individuals depicted in the photos, both on the cover and throughout this book, are only models.

Cover Photo: iStock.com/ParkerDeen

Dollar Photo Club: 10 Monkey Business; 12 JcJg Photography; 13 Rob; 19 robert lerich; 23 Monkey Business; 27 krutoeva; 28 WavebreakmediaMicro; 32 nikkytok; 34 kolotype; 37 kolinko_tanya; 38 vbaleha; 41 Barabas Attila; 42 patrick. **iStock.com:** 18 selvanegra; 24 monkeybusinessimages; 30 Razvan; 40 poco_bw. **Wikimedia Commons:** 11 Open Clip Art; 15 Saltanat ebli; 20 Garrondo.